Learning to *Love* *without Losing* *Yourself*

9 Steps to Healthy Boundaries and Fulfilling Relationships

Cover & Interior designer: Van Canque

While the author has made every effort to provide accurate contact information at the time of publication, neither the author nor the publisher is responsible for errors, or for changes that occur after publication. Further, the publisher does not have any control over and does not assume any responsibility for author or third-party websites or their content.

Relationship Academy Publishing
7061 W. North Ave., #270
Oak Park, IL., 60302

Cataloging-in-Publication Data is on file with the Library of Congress

Hardcover ISBN: 978-1-7369335-0-3
Paperback ISBN: 978-1-7369335-1-0
Ebook ISBN: 978-1-7369335-2-7

1st edition, April 2021

Printed in the United States of America

Disclaimer: *This book is designed to provide accurate and authoritative information regarding the subject matter covered. By its sale, neither the publisher nor the author is engaged in rendering psychological or other professional services. If expert assistance or counseling is needed, the services of a competent professional should be sought.*

"There are two primary choices in life: to accept conditions as they exist, or accept the responsibility for changing them. "

—Denis Waitley

Contents

Introduction

Is a lack of boundaries a major issue in your life?

Do you feel overwhelmed with guilt whenever you choose to prioritize yourself?

If you answered 'yes' to both questions, then you're not alone. Many people struggle with setting healthy boundaries, whether it's because of their compulsive people-pleasing habit or because they fear rejection and abandonment.

While there are many reasons why you found yourself in this situation right now, if you've picked up this book then you must have realized you're stuck and in order for you to get 'unstuck', something has got to give.

You may be frustrated with your inability to say 'no' or you might be resentful of your codependency and separation anxiety. You may feel exhausted, angry, damaged, broken, and at your wit's end. Understand that everyone goes through hardships, whether on the same scale, bigger, or smaller.

Overcoming these issues will take a lot of time, effort, and energy on your part. The journey will be long and strenuous, but if you stick around to the finish line, you will find the rewards to be more than worthwhile.

In this book, we will first delve into all the specifics of boundaries, what they are, their different types, how to tell if you have them or not, the differences between rigid, loose, and healthy boundaries, how to establish and reinforce your own rules, as well as how to deal with violations.

Moreover, we will also discuss the importance of saying 'no', and how you can learn to decline or reject other people's demands without apologizing. You can also expect some self-exploration in regards to why you're constantly choosing others over yourself, how you can overcome this codependency, and how you can begin to separate your stuff from others' stuff.

So ultimately, you will be able to set the process of self-acceptance in motion and learn how to honor your true, authentic self. To make this transition, you will need to build strong, clear, and consistent boundaries that you will then work actively on reinforcing.

This book will help you put an end to the perennial struggle and mental turmoil you've been going through for years, if not decades. Once you start seeing the value in unapologetically being yourself and knowing your worth, this will allow you to overcome the guilt and get rid of those self-limiting beliefs that have always held you down.

So finally you can learn to redirect that energy you've dejectedly spent on others and focus it on the people that matter and experiences that will let you grow, spread your wings, and liberate yourself from the restraints of low self-esteem and self-doubts.

So are you ready to take back control of your life?

"When we fail to set boundaries and hold people accountable, we feel used and mistreated. This is why we sometimes attack who they are, which is far more hurtful than addressing a behavior or a choice."

— Brené Brown,

Chapter 1

Step 1: What Are Boundaries?

Pause a moment, take a deep breath, and reflect on your life until now, all the choices you've made, all the steps you've taken, each and every action that led you to this very moment, to who you are, to what you've become. We're going to start this chapter by asking yourself the hard questions. Yes, you're exhausted, yes, you're undervalued, overlooked, and even unheard in most of your relationships, whether it be a romantic partner, a friend, a family member, a boss, or even a coworker.

You find yourself constantly apologizing for the inconvenience you're causing, the discomfort, the disregard. You're sorry for this thing and that thing, you're sorry for the space you occupy, for the air you breathe, you're sorry you exist. You're always accommodating everyone around you, making sure they all feel acknowledged and recognized, making sure they're comfortable and happy.

You're always on the go, you're always worrying, overthinking the most minute of details. "Did I offend them when I said that?", "I hope they don't think I resent them because I refused the snacks they offered", "maybe they're angry at me, I must have done something, they seemed mad" … This might sound too idle or insignificant to some people, but finding yourself in this spot, you know how much weight this holds in your life.

A 'weird' look from someone can send you spiraling for hours, thinking of every encounter you've ever had with that person, every word you've uttered in their presence, and every action you've taken. Then you get tangled up into a vicious cycle of re-examining and re-evaluating those experiences to gauge what you have done that might have rubbed them off the wrong way. You're constantly trying to keep everyone around you happy, satisfied, and fulfilled. You always go out of your way to ensure they remain that way.

You obsess over what you can do that will make their lives easier. Whatever free time you have, you spend pondering over the possibility that the people in your life secretly hate you. Despite your efforts to show them how much you love and appreciate them, it never feels enough, you're always tormenting yourself because you're convinced you can offer them more than what you already have.

You try and try and try to be nice to everyone, to never hurt anyone, to put other people's needs way above your own. You give your all to the people around you, sometimes even those that aren't necessarily part of your close circle. You're guilty, all the time. You've been brought up to revere others, constantly told to indulge everyone else, to do whatever you're told, to be obedient, you've been taught that your feelings don't matter, that others always come first.

So you venerate the savoir-vivre bible you've been assigned and you live by the holiness of etiquette and diplomacy. You often find yourself playing the role of mediator, you think every time you leave the house conflict will arise, and things will escalate, that you won't be there to de-escalate the situation, that it will snowball into a massive issue, that something bad might happen.

From the moment you wake up until you go to bed, you're immersed in that caregiver role. You allow others to cut in line, you give your turn to someone else at the doctor's office despite you being in the waiting room for 2 consecutive hours, yet you think they deserve it more, that they're probably sicker than you are, you give permission to others to walk all over you, you're always prepared to be at their beck and call, you have a hard time rejecting other people's demands, so you never say no, unless it's to yourself, then you always do.

You're quick to deny yourself even the smallest of pleasures. You're convinced you're not worthy of the attention and care that you're constantly investing in your relationships. You're aware of this, you realize the patterns in your behavior, you know very well that you're giving too much, that you ought to be stronger, that you should stand your ground more often, establish boundaries, and set healthier coping habits, yet you feel utterly stuck in the position you're currently at, it goes beyond a personal trait or a quirk of yours, it's become your whole identity.

It feels as if you've dug your own grave, and now you're lying in it, soil falling over your head in slow motion, as passersby take advantage of your kindness, as the people who matter to you the most are languidly eating away at you, your tenderness, your compassion, and your empathy. They're depleting you of your energy and spirit without even realizing it. And what do you do?

You say nothing, you apologize for the unconsumed rotting parts of yourself, then you apologize for the gruesome imagery, and you offer something to remedy the smell. Despite the reassurances you get, although few in quantity, you still think that deep down, you're the problem. You're so quick to blame yourself even for something as out of your reach and as unpredictable as the weather.

You can somehow paint yourself as the perpetrator and culprit in any conflict that ever occurred in the history of your existence. You're so forgiving of others, so lenient, so accommodating, but never with yourself, never in a million years. You keep replaying past experiences inside your head, wishing you'd done more, then maybe they would have stayed, then maybe they wouldn't have left.

You realize the contradictory thoughts and ideas inside your brain, you can clearly see the dichotomy between what is ratio-nal and what isn't, you're willing to completely absolve others yet you put yourself at the highest, most impossible-to-reach, standards, knowing that you will fail, yet also being convinced of the fact that you failed because you didn't try hard enough.

So what happens next is you punish yourself for your deficiencies, for your flaws, for your failures, for your shortcomings, you beat yourself up for being such a pushover, a people pleaser, a weakling, as you spiral deeper and deeper into the rabbit hole. You wish you could be more assertive; you fantasize about telling your boss off, about giving a piece of your mind to that nosy co-worker or standing up to your berating mother.

You realize that if you were a bit more assertive, you would have a bit more room to take care of your own needs. So what about you? What about what you want? When are you going to become the protagonist in your own life? How do you feel about the life you're currently leading? What do you think is missing from it? What kind of present do you want to create for yourself?

You probably don't have a very clear idea or vision of what you really want. You're so hung up on keeping everyone else happy that you never stopped to ask yourself these questions. It never even crossed your mind to consider what you truly want in life. Like everyone else, you've had dreams and aspirations, but you managed to brush those under the rug to make room for the 'priorities', or what you think matters more.

But now is the time to put everything out in the open. If you've picked up this book then you're tired of putting other people's wants and needs above yours. You're ready to explore other options, even if you're not sure what that really means, at least not yet. So let me ask you this, how would you define boundaries? What first comes to mind when you think of being assertive?

Based on your reasoning, this might suggest a certain degree of bluntness, saying whatever is on your mind, being rude, telling people off, or showing no regard, nor consideration to others whatsoever. You may even associate it with yelling and slamming doors. Though this couldn't be farther from the truth.

Assertiveness is many things... It's the ability to speak your mind without reservations or aggressivity. It's the ability to clearly communicate your desires and needs without feeling like you have to somehow defend or justify yourself. It's having the courage and confidence to unapologetically be who you are. It's standing up for yourself as well as others, it's expressing your thoughts and opinions, it's the ability to say no and honor that no.

If you want to truly understand what boundaries are so you can start implementing those into your life and taking back control, you must be ready to leave your assumptions and misconceptions at the door. You can't walk into this expecting to maintain the pre-made ideas you have constructed, because those are exactly what led you to this point.

So let's explore what boundaries are and how you can identify the different types of boundaries as well as boundary violations.

What is a Boundary

According to the Merriam-Webster Dictionary, a boundary is "something that indicates or fixes a limit or extent". So perhaps the most literal understanding of what a boundary is, is that limit that indicates the extent of a property, where it ends and where it begins.

In this context, a 'no trespassing' sign indicates the outcome of prosecution if that line is crossed, and that boundary is violated. These physical boundaries are very easy to understand because they involve concrete elements like the land itself or the sign.

On the other hand, personal boundaries are vaguer than this, hence, harder to understand. Since they depend on several factors like the setting or the people you're with. Not only that, but they're also unique to each individual in particular. So what could be a limit for you might not translate as the same for someone else.

What a Boundary is and What a Boundary isn't

Many people who struggle with distinguishing responsibilities and taking ownership in their lives, find themselves lacking proper boundaries. This issue is due to a large misconception of what boundaries truly are. So when told to set these limits or even attempt to, they find it impossible to do without seeming like a hostile or unfriendly person.

Furthermore, establishing legitimate boundaries becomes a source of fear and anxiety more than a catalyst for freedom and self-respect. "What if other people are upset, hurt, or offended by my boundaries?", "What if it makes me look selfish?", "How can I be assertive when someone asks something of me that I'm not comfortable with?", "How do I say no to someone without being rude or feeling guilty?".

These are all good questions to raise and address. Though we will delve into some of those in more detail later on, for now, here's what a boundary is and what a boundary is not.

Boundaries are:
- **Healthy**
- **Mandatory**
- **Respectful**
- **Considerate**
- **Biblical**

Boundaries are not:
- **Selfish**
- **Disrespectful**
- **Sinful**

- **Dismissive**
- **Shameful**

When parents bring up their children in an environment where discussing emotions and feelings is considered a hindrance rather than an opportunity for growth, they're inherently teaching them that whatever they think they feel isn't valid. Subsequently, saying no becomes frowned upon within these dysfunctional families. So in this way, the children learn to internalize their feelings and to suppress them deep inside.

Other people become the center of their existence, as they're taught that everyone else is always right, yet they never are. Sending them defenseless without the slightest notion of what healthy boundaries are, without the ability to formulate their thoughts and opinions or to stand up for themselves, and straight into a world of manipulation, control, and exploitation, means they believe that others can do what they please with them.

Then unfolds the slippery slope of discarding their needs and ignoring their own rights in favor of other people's. So the child's mind becomes a festering ground for negative thoughts, aggressivity, low self-esteem, lack of confidence, passivity, and painful memories.

In order to grow from this perennial mindset, we must identify our rights and needs and choose to respect them time and time again. Taking care of ourselves in all of our relationships and overcoming these negative thoughts and habits is a process that takes time, effort, and energy.

This is the only way to give room to our true self to emerge and flourish. Through establishing healthy boundaries, we also outline limits to keep up safe, a kind of safety perhaps, that was never experienced before. But before we begin setting healthy boundaries, we must first understand the various types of boundaries and what purpose each of them serves.

Types of Boundaries

Knowing our personal limits, as well as negotiables and non-negotiables, helps define who we are and influence all aspects of our lives. With that said, by the time we get to adulthood, we're so tangled up in all of our responsibilities and duties that we fail to recognize the intangible boundaries that govern our daily lives. To remedy that, we need to understand our limits whether personal and relational, intellectual, sexual, physical, psychological, or emotional.

1.   Personal/Relational Boundaries

Personal or relational boundaries are those that dictate where you end and where others begin. This often includes both the physical and emotional space you establish between yourself and those surrounding you. These rules and guidelines help you distinguish what's acceptable from others and what's not, in terms of communication, interaction, and behavior.

For instance, someone with healthy boundaries is capable of saying 'no' to people when they feel inclined to, but that doesn't mean they can't open up or allow themselves the intimacy of close relationships. So the type of personal boundaries you set or don't dictates how healthy or unhealthy your relationships are.

2.   Intellectual Boundaries

Intellectual boundaries focus on thoughts and ideas and curiosity. So well-balanced intellectual boundaries entail respect for other people's ideas in addition to a general awareness of what is considered appropriate for discussion by all parties.

These intellectual boundaries are violated when someone's thoughts and ideas are dismissed, belittled, or completely shut down. Respect and a disposition to dialogue are important aspects of maintaining one's intellectual boundaries.

Moreover, these limits also include considerations of when it's adequate to talk about a particular topic and when it isn't. However, this does not mean that you need to embrace all thoughts, opinions, and perspectives. Again, when we tie intellectual boundaries to personal ones, this gives us a clearer understanding of what is acceptable and what is simply offensive.

In this context, it's important to acknowledge the distinction between healthy and unhealthy discourse. For example, if somebody is sharing a harmful opinion, i.e- sexism, racism, homophobia, etc- then you have every right to stand your ground and draw the line.

Establish an intellectual boundary in whatever way you see fit, whether that's letting them know you don't tolerate those views, distancing yourself from the person, or cutting them off entirely. Don't feel obliged to engage in 'intellectual' discussions with someone who clearly violates those boundaries.

3.   Sexual Boundaries

Sexual boundaries consist of the intellectual, emotional, and physical elements of sexuality. Healthy sexual boundaries involve consent, respect, agreement, understanding of preferences, and aversions, as well as privacy. This entails a level of mutual understanding and respect of sexual desires and limitations between partners.

Namely, asking for consent before engaging in sexual acts, discussing contraception, protecting the privacy of the other person, inquiring about what they like and dislike, saying 'no' to things you don't want to do, etc.

Violation of these boundaries occurs when there are unwanted sexual advances or comments, unsolicited touching, the pressure to perform sexual acts, lying about one's health history or contraception usage, leering, criticizing the other person's sexual preferences, etc.

4.   Physical Boundaries

Physical boundaries involve the need for personal space and comfort with physical touch. Having healthy physical boundaries means there's an inherent awareness of what is deemed appropriate and what isn't based on the setting and type of relationship, e.g: hugging, kissing, shaking hands, etc.

So a violation of these physical boundaries could be an invasion of personal space, i.e someone going through your belongings, or being touched inappropriately when you don't want to. These violations can vary in degree, from mild to severe. Mild being someone entering your room without permission and severe being serious physical abuse, harassment, or neglect.

5.   Psychological/Emotional Boundaries

Psychological and emotional boundaries refer to our emotions, our perception of ourselves, as well as our perception of others. It's a combination of the knowledge, experience, reflections, memories, and assumptions that we carry in our minds but also the lies we feed ourselves. Healthy psychological boundaries are supposed to protect our identity, self-worth, and self-esteem.

Establishing these emotional boundaries helps us determine how much we're capable of taking in. In addition to that, it also allows us to understand when it's appropriate to share our emotions when it isn't, and with whom. Respecting these boundaries entails a mutual recognition and validation of emotions, as well as an assessment of one's ability to take in that emotional information.

The following questions will help you get a better understanding of your emotional boundaries or lack thereof.

- **Do you take responsibility for your feelings, emotions, and needs?**
- **Do you let others take responsibility for theirs?**
- **Do you feel responsible for other people's feelings, emotions, and needs to the extent of neglecting yours?**
- **Do you know when to say 'no', and are you capable of**

saying it?

- **Can you ask for what you need?**
- **Are you constantly seeking to please others but never yourself?**
- **Do your feelings depend on the feelings of those around you?**
- **Do you become upset just because the people surrounding you are upset?**
- **Do you tend to adopt other people's opinions and views as your own?**

The answers you provide will help you determine how strong, or weak, your emotional and psychological boundaries are. If you find that you're most often influenced and controlled by the feelings, emotions, and negative thoughts of people around you, then your emotional boundaries are more porous than you think.

6.   Spiritual Boundaries

Establishing healthy boundaries starts with recognizing what is within our control and what is well beyond our reach. We can't replace destructive habits and undo the damage our spirits have been subjected to if we fail to recognize our human limitations.

This type of boundary is essential, yet it's seldom a subject of discussion. For starters, it's incredibly hard to lead compassionate, loving, and just lives when all of those characteristics are buried deep under all the toxic emotional pain, negativity, and heartache.

Maintaining healthy spiritual boundaries is an integral part of leading a fulfilling life. In many ways, spirituality is a necessary refuge, a place to find solace, and realize the complexity of the universe. While some people may not deem faith to be important, others recognize it as a critical element in their lives.

It's what helps them stay grounded and what provides guidance, comfort, and peace when the world feels like it's crumbling down. Whichever side you stand with, setting healthy spiritual boundaries means you're able to recognize the spiritual beliefs others hold without criticizing them or belittling their convictions.

This doesn't mean adopting their beliefs as your own in the same way you wouldn't want them to push their spiritual realizations on you, judge you because you don't follow their scriptures, or tell you how to live your life according to their faith.

This goes both ways, of course, and although boundaries are harder to delineate when it comes to the spiritual world, you can, nevertheless, rely on your words and actions to create and set these protective fences.

7. Time Boundaries

Time boundaries, just like the name indicates, are those boundaries that govern the way you spend your time as well as how much of your time you allow others to take. Healthy time boundaries mean you're aware of your priorities and you allocate enough time to each aspect of your life accordingly, whether it be job responsibilities, relationships, chores, hobbies, exercise, meditation, or prayer. These time boundaries are usually violated when you neglect to dedicate a portion of your day to one of your priorities or when another person disregards your needs, duties, and demand too much of your time.

8. Material Boundaries

Material boundaries involve money, possessions, assets, and other material belongings. Having healthy material boundaries means you're capable of setting and respecting the limits on what you will share and who you will share it with. For instance, you may find it appropriate to lend your car to a close family member or friend, but not to an acquaintance or someone you met recently. These boundaries are violated when a person is coerced to lend or give something they own, but also when that person's belongings and possessions are stolen, damaged, or misplaced.

Rigid Boundaries vs. Porous Boundaries

Most people have a combination of various types of boundaries. While they could have healthy boundaries at work, this might not be the case in their romantic relationships, or with their family. A person who has rigid boundaries typically has very few close relationships, is very protective of their thoughts, feelings, and opinions, and usually avoids all forms of intimacy.

In addition to that, they're often detached from others, even with their significant other, and they go out of their way to avoid rejection by keeping others at a distance. These people live by self-sufficiency and never ask for help, even when they truly need it.

On the other hand, a person who has loose or porous boundaries is often guilty of oversharing personal information even if it's to people they've just met. Moreover, a person with porous boundaries often has difficulty saying 'no' to other people's requests, as they fear rejection if they don't comply with everybody else.

These people are very dependent on the opinions of those around them and they tend to accept abuse or disrespect because they feel as if they deserve it. Furthermore, they feel responsible for other people's feelings so they're constantly in need of reassurance. These two types of people are often referred to as the sword and the doormat.

Someone who assumes a 'doormat' stance in their daily life is often controlled either by people surrounding them or by their own thoughts, feelings, and emotions. They don't want to disappoint others and their attempts at pleasing everyone is often a way for them to seek validation, reassurance, and love. Moreover, a person with a doormat stance may be afraid of assertiveness for fear of shame, rejection, or destabilization of their personal relationships.

While the doormat outlook is weaker or more passive, the sword relies on power and strength (although temporary). Think of it in terms of battle or war, a person holding a sword is most likely nervous and willing to preserve and protect themselves at all costs.

They're already on the defensive as they try to keep others at a distance, and they may even have intentions of hurting others. Underneath all the pretense, the self-worth of a 'sword person' is threatened as they never truly feel emotionally safe.

When disagreements occur, they're often quick to attack and display aggressive or hostile behavior. Taking a sword stance means pushing others away regardless of their intentions, which produces alienation and disconnection with the people in their lives.

"When you notice someone does something toxic the first time, don't wait for the second time before you address it or cut them off.
Many survivors are used to the "wait and see" tactic which only leaves them vulnerable to a second attack. As your boundaries get stronger, the wait time gets shorter. You never have to justify your intuition."

— Shahida Arabi

Chapter 2

Step 2: How Do You Know You Have Boundaries?

In the previous chapter, we've thoroughly examined the different types of boundaries, what they are, what they aren't, and the different categories you can expect to work on during your boundary-setting journey.

In this chapter, we discuss why you need boundaries, then we move into the 10 different signs that you lack proper boundaries, as well as some common misconceptions and myths surrounding these boundaries.

At the end of this chapter, you will be able to distinguish between the areas where you've managed to successfully establish healthy rules and which areas remain lacking in that regard. In addition to that, we will also explore the benefits and rewards you can expect from standing your ground and laying a good foundation for a more fulfilling life.

Why Do You Need Boundaries?

Boundaries are an essential part of producing and reflecting a healthy self-image. When a person has strong healthy boundaries, they implicitly communicate confidence and self-respect to the world. Further, this goes to show that they're aware of their worth and they can clearly demonstrate their value.

Healthy boundaries not only make us feel good about ourselves but they also protect our personal integrity. If you don't set and maintain healthy boundaries, you're practically telling others that you're at their mercy.

So in a way you allow them to dictate your thoughts, feelings, emotions, and behavior. In addition to that, having weak or nonexistent boundaries also means you tend to invest all of your time and energy doing what others want you to do or tell you to do.

Never saying no eventually leads to feelings of loss, frustration, and unfulfillment. Without proper boundaries, we tend to confuse our needs and desires with those of people around us. This confusion results in codependency and one-sided relationships.

Hence why it is impossible to enjoy meaningful friendships or romance in healthy relationships without clear personal boundaries. Not only that but when a person doesn't have an apparent idea of what their limits are, they become subject to heightened stress and intense feelings of hopelessness.

Because they have a penchant toward overcommitting to everything and everyone, they often find themselves exhausted and drained of all energy due to how mentally constantly taxing pleasing others is. This either unfolds as burnout or a nervous breakdown, and neither options are ideal.

A lack of personal boundaries also entails a person to feel worthless, weak, and never good enough. Then doubt and self-loathing creep in and the ability to voice their truth and communicate their needs verges on the impossible. This is why setting healthy boundaries is so important and why it matters so much.

10 Signs You Lack Healthy Boundaries

If you're not sure whether your boundaries are strong and adequate or whether they serve your needs, here are 10 signs that can be greatly indicative of too rigid or too porous boundaries.

1.   You find it hard to make a decision

Without healthy boundaries, you often find yourself listening to other people or even seeking them for their opinions. First, you have your friend who's convinced you of what they would do if they were in your shoes. Then, you have your mother that completely disagrees with your friend.

Between the two, you find yourself at an impasse, incapable, almost paralyzed to decide on one thing or the other. However, you keep listening to the people surrounding you, even at your own peril, giving them the power to make such decisive moves on your behalf.

So you spend your whole life doing what this or that person told you to do until you lose all sense of self and identity. When you don't have healthy boundaries, you're so focused on everyone else that you can't even recognize what you want, so when faced with several choices, you go completely blank.

2.   You hate to disappoint others

Perhaps you've been called a people pleaser or a pushover before, and despite how much that must have hurt, you're still incapable of saying no or uttering an opinion that slightly disagrees with that of another person around you.

When you lack healthy boundaries, you're constantly thinking of the needs, wants, and desires of the people in your life. So much so that those concerns completely overshadow your own needs and wants. You go out of your way to satisfy other people even if it's done at your expense and at the expense of your sanity and well-being.

So you go along with everybody's plans, you accept their opinions despite how harmful they might be, you embrace the disrespect and abuse because you'd much rather struggle with stress and anxiety than to disappoint others or let them down in some way.

3.   You suffer from guilt and anxiety

Many people who struggle with establishing healthy boundaries often find themselves responsible for how others around them feel. For instance, if others aren't happy, they take it too personally, even if they have nothing to do with the reason why that person is upset in the first place.

So they feel guilty for the smallest things, something as trivial as taking the last slice of pizza or asking someone to move along the sofa so they can sit too.

This ongoing guilt can become quite unbearable, especially when you feel accountable for the comfort and happiness of everybody around you. The guilt is such an insurmountable weight to hold on one's shoulders at all times, which is why boundaries are crucial.

4.   You either overshare or undershare

When you have too loose and porous boundaries, you tend to overshare intimate details and personal information to just about anyone, from your mailman to the barista serving you coffee. While exchanging pleasantries is a nice way to make conversation with people you've just met, telling them about your private life will only leave you vulnerable to hurt, control, manipulation, and pain.

You're practically giving away your personal story to somebody who might use your flaws and weaknesses against you. On the other hand, when your boundaries are too rigid, you often push other people away despite their best attempts to get close to you and get you to open up and share your feelings.

That's part of the problem too since you constantly build all these walls and fences around you, you involuntarily engage in the process of losing touch with the real world. In this way, you also relinquish the know-how of openly discussing your thoughts and emotions.

With that said, having healthy boundaries means you have a deep awareness of when it is appropriate to share what information with whom. So this gives you more control over the details of your private life and who gets to learn about them as well as in what context.

5.   You're often exhausted or drained of energy

Always being at the beck and call of everyone in your life and constantly doing what they want means you have little space for much else. So you're left to cram your own priorities, responsibilities, and indulgences in the leftover time you have.

This, again, is a clear violation of time boundaries. Because you have little time to fulfill all your daily tasks, you tend to sacrifice other things like proper sleep, balanced meals, or self-care practices in order to accomplish all the 'priorities' on your list.

As a result, leading such a hectic life can make you chronically fatigued, exhausted, and drained of all energy or enthusiasm. So at the end of the day, you have no room to identify and pursue your personal dreams or passions because you're always catering to everybody else's needs.

6.   You're annoyed and irritable most of the time

Going along with everything other people are doing can be exhausting, but it can also be a detrimental source of resentment and frustration. This is especially prevalent when those around you don't share the same values and worldview. So living through what can only be described as a contradiction is bound to take a toll on your mood and mental health.

On one side you're convinced that whatever the other person does is wrong, on the other side, you're too afraid to say anything for fear of rejection. Internalizing these feelings results in a slow yet gradual build-up of irritation and bitterness. You might be wondering why you always feel on edge or on the bridge of a meltdown, and a lack of healthy boundaries is the answer.

Because you can't get yourself to voice your truth without the guilt that is sure to follow, you say nothing, and your anger rises. This is in addition to always worrying about what others think or might think in juxtaposition with the remorse of what you secretly want. Accordingly, going against everything you believe in will end up in feelings of hopelessness and anguish over time.

7.   You have an intense fear of rejection or abandonment
Poor boundary setting can often be traced back to early childhood when you were taught that not doing what others want you to do would result in rejection and abandonment. Attention, love, and care are important for children, so your subconscious may have connected the dots in this way: in order for you, as a child, to get that attention and love, you need to go along with what others want.

While not having boundaries as a child might have worked out well, or at least a bit in your favor, as an adult, your fears and worries of being forgotten and discarded have not managed to dissipate with age, in fact, they might be even stronger with a more robust grasp on your mind. So based on your reasoning, you think that being boundary-less will lead to affection and tenderness when in reality, it will only lead to loneliness and complex relationships.

In this regard, establishing healthy boundaries will allow you to still feel loved and cared for even when you don't want to do what other people around you want you to. One variable doesn't have to be dependent on the other, you can say 'no' to a person, and that won't affect how much they love you or appreciate you as a friend, mother, wife, sister, daughter, cousin, niece, and so on.

8.   Your relationships tend to foster difficulties and drama
When you don't set and communicate clear boundaries to others, whether family members, friends, or romantic partners, you're practically promoting the fact that you don't know your worth nor how to take care of yourself. This sends the wrong signals and attracts people who will try to control and manipulate you. They will not only try to get you to submit to their whims and inclinations but also propel you to turn your life upside down until it conforms to their standards and perceptions.

At one given moment, you might be too frustrated with their manipulative tendencies, you might feel like they're suffocating you or like they're constantly watching your every move ready to jump in and criticize how you manage everything, so at this point, you might tip the balance, switch roles, and start to secretly plant some thoughts here and there in order to control them and get under their skin the same way they did with you.

Neither sword nor doormat will prevail in this scenario. In other words, not setting healthy boundaries will affect the nature of your relationships to the point where they're too dysfunctional and deeply rooted in a codependent system. So the worst-case scenario will entail that you end up at the receiving end of verbal, emotional, physical, or sexual abuse.

9.   You make too many sacrifices at your own expense
When you feel responsible for other people's feelings and needs, you also feel like you should be the one to constantly make sacrifices in order to keep them happy, whether it be your mother, your friend, your significant other, your boss, or colleague. The tremendously popular idealized image of women as intrinsic caregivers, as people who are always ready and willing to sacrifice themselves for the sake of others at all costs, doesn't help either.

Though, ironically, if you were to set healthy boundaries, you'd be much more effective in meeting the needs of those you feel responsible for. While self-sacrifice can be a vital part of being a parent for instance, if not balanced with healthy boundaries and the ability to communicate your thoughts and needs, these expectations can become a huge obstacle to your self-expression, emotional health, and overall well-being.

Making too many sacrifices at your own expense leaves you open to harm, disrespect, blame-shifting, and abasement. When someone hurts you, instead of letting them know you don't approve of the way they're treating you, you might feel worse for their pain than you do for the impact their words and actions had on you.

So you choose to make them feel better rather than dealing with your fear of rejection and abandonment. While making sacrifices is an inherent part of parenthood and other relationships, but it should never be at the expense of your own health, both mental and physical, as well as your well-being.

10.   You're passive-aggressive

When you're constantly the victim of other people's caprices and impulses, you start to feel powerless and unable to make your own decisions. As you slowly turn into a passive viewer rather than the main character in your own life, feelings of anger, frustration, and resentment begin to surface, slowly, then all at once.

So much so that the only way you can silence those furious thoughts is by making a drastic change. Continuously feeling upset and disempowered will lead you to try and manipulate back that control, energy, and power you lost by complaining, nagging, or even punishing those around you in little ways. In addition to that, you might also blame others for your failures and all that went wrong in your life.

This is mainly because you played along and went with what they wanted rather than what you secretly desired. So without healthy boundaries, your passive aggression will worsen and you will never realize that you're the one who's responsible for your own life, that it's not something you leave up to chance or give others the power to do whatever they please with it.

Why do you suffer from weak boundaries?

Before you go ahead and blame yourself for yet another aspect of your life that is out of control, take a moment to recognize that your weak and porous boundaries are not entirely a result of your own doing. While it's not your fault that you lack healthy boundaries, it is your responsibility to now developing these self-preserving barriers.

Allow yourself the compassion and understanding that you so readily give to others because you deserve that self-love just as much, if not more than those around you. So why do you suffer from weak boundaries? To answer this question, you need to go far back in the past so you can unearth the roots of these patterns.

As a child, you probably had little to no control over what your parents, teachers, and other adults taught you. In most cases, those with weak to non-existent boundaries were set a bad illustration of what healthy boundaries are like.

Observing the dysfunctional and codependent dynamic within one's family is a great contributor to this issue, especially when the person is taught time and time again that love equals what they do and not who they are.

Because the first role models you had, as a child, were your parents and family members, a reflection and close examination of that environment is much overdue. So consider the following questions to determine whether what you were taught as a child has impacted your views on boundary setting.

- **What hints and messages did your siblings, parents, and other authority figures send you when you were a child?**
- **Were you only shown love and affection when you went along with what your parents wanted you to do?**
- **Were you only rewarded and praised when you went out of your way, sacrificing your needs and desires for those of someone else's?**
- **Were you punished and grounded for saying 'no'? Was it the same when you spoke up or talked back?**
- **Did you feel responsible and compelled to take care of another adult -a parent perhaps?**

If your answers are positive for the most part, then this is a sign that you were brought up thinking a lack of boundaries and complete obedience are a good thing.

Common myths and misconceptions about boundaries

If you struggle with setting and keeping healthy boundaries, then you probably carry a number of myths and misconceptions that have been passed down to you or that you've been conditioned to believe. So here are some common myths that you need to be aware of.

1.   Boundaries are selfish

You want to be generous, giving, and thoughtful, so more often than not, saying no to others sounds selfish and entitled. However, this couldn't be farther from the truth. Don't you think it's selfish to ask others to go out of their way to please you, despite how distressing that might be for them? It goes the same for the other way around too!

You can't keep allowing that guilt and fear of abandonment, rejection, and anger to rule your life. Boundaries will not cancel out your compassion and empathy towards others, and they won't make you egotistic or self-centered. On the contrary, people who have healthy boundaries have a higher ability to care for others.

Being selfish means "seeking or concentrating on one's own advantage, pleasure, or well-being without regard for others" (Merriam-Webster). A lot of people tend to confuse egoism with stewardship. So what you need to understand is that meeting your own needs is not a luxury or a pleasure that you indulge in occasionally, it's rather a responsibility that you owe to yourself.

2. Boundaries will cause your relationships to suffer

If you're already involved in a codependent relationship, then beginning to establish boundaries will inevitably generate awkward and troublesome waves of change. You will most certainly be met with resistance and reluctance or utter refusal to accept these newly-developed limits. This is particularly prominent in people who've had weak to absent boundaries for their whole lives.

With that said, you shouldn't see boundaries as offensive instruments or something you use to hurt others. Far from it, boundaries are meant to be used as a defensive instrument to protect you from control, manipulation, abuse, and just being walked all over by other people.

While saying no to someone may cause some degree of discomfort, contrary to your belief, it won't injure them to the point of no return, and they won't suddenly hate you in secret either. Be that as it may, this principle doesn't concern only that share of people that are toxic or harmful, it also includes those with valid needs and issues.

Sometimes, you simply can't afford to make sacrifices to help another person for one reason or the other, no matter how legitimate. When faced with these situations, you have to allow the people around you to take responsibility for their own actions. You, like anyone else, are human, you have your own needs, your own problems, your own difficulties.

So just like you wouldn't expect all of your friends to be available at all times, they should also understand that you have a life of your own, you have a busy schedule, you need some time alone, or time to unwind. Hence why any well-balanced and supportive relationships will not only flourish but also encourage the establishment of healthy boundaries.

3.   Boundaries will make you unhappy or cause others to hate you

This is a common concern that involves both setting boundaries and being on the receiving end of other people's boundaries. When you begin to delineate your limits, particularly after a long time of not doing so, you will be consumed by worry and anxiety.

The anxiety that others may not take your boundaries well, that everyone will suddenly resent you for saying no, that they will talk behind your back and say how prudish or strict of a person you've become. While that's a valid concern, anyone who actually thinks of you to be too rigid or too blunt is NOT your responsibility.

You're not meant to oversee everybody else's lives, you're in control of yours and that's where it ends, or should end. This doesn't mean you should be rude about your wants and needs, but you shouldn't apologize for those either. You worry about not being liked, you think that your life will be miserable if people hate or resent you.

But that's the thing, you're not meant to be loved and adored by just about anyone and everyone. You can't be the hero of everyone around you. You can't take away all of their pain, solve all their problems, or make them happy and fulfilled with their own lives. You can't make them love themselves or start to treat themselves better, with more respect.

All you can do is love the people around you who are worthy of your love -if they outright reject your boundaries, then they're not worth your time. Now, on the other hand, you could very well think that boundaries will make you unhappy because you've been told 'no' so many times that you would hate to put someone else in the receiving end of rejection.

For instance, you might take it too personally when a person cannot help you or go along with your perspective. So when they display their disagreement, you take it to heart, you get offended and you think they mean it as an attack against you or your reasoning.

In a similar fashion, by not setting boundaries, you think you will be happier because you will never personally offend anyone or refuse their requests. Even so, what will make you miserable is having to be available at all times for everyone in your life.

This is no way to help anyone else, not until you start with yourself first. You can't be giving, compassionate, and caring if you're exhausted and angry all the time. Healthy boundaries will help you lead a happy and fulfilling life, and as a result, you'll be more inclined to help and meet the needs of those around you.

4.   Boundaries are fixed

You might have the misconception that boundaries are fixed and set in stone, that once you decide on a limit and you put it to practice, you can't go back on your word or change your mind. On the contrary, boundaries are not rigid, they're not unbending, they're merely there to protect you and your needs, whatever those might be, whether for now or further in the future.

Just like you're not immobile or stagnant, you shouldn't expect your boundaries to be static either. You're a human being, you make mistakes, you fall, you get back up, you grow, you learn from past experiences, you're subject to continuous development. The same goes for your boundaries!

What you might be comfortable with now, could become a source of objection in the future, and vice versa, so healthy boundaries need to be flexible. As long as you value your own opinions, know how to communicate your thoughts and feelings, and don't compromise your principles for others, then your boundaries are your own and they ought to be respected.

Perhaps you have reservations about setting a boundary with a friend, for instance, then changing your mind later on, and not knowing how to broach the subject with said friend. Again, boundaries can always be renegotiated and you have every right to change them when you find yourself in a safer environment.

It's important that you understand the fact that you own your boundaries, they don't own you! You've created those boundaries, and they're only there as long as they serve their purpose, which is to protect you. So in some context where you no longer need that protection, you may renegotiate your limits in light of these circumstances.

How do you know you have healthy boundaries?

Not everyone knows what their boundaries are. If you're codependent, for instance, then you might not have many boundaries, to begin with. In addition to that, you might also confuse what your boundaries really are with what others expect of you. So if you're not sure you've set good boundaries or any at all, ask yourself the following questions.

- **Do I feel stressed out, overwhelmed, burned out?**
- **Would I do almost anything to avoid hurting others?**
- **Do I feel as if my children, partner, parents, or friends run my life?**
- **Do I often feel as if my life isn't my own?**
- **Do I feel taken advantage of by those I love?**

- Do I resent others for being too demanding and at times inconsiderate?
- Do I feel like I deserve respect? Or do I feel like I have to earn it?
- Do others' needs seem more urgent than mine?
- Do I tend to meet others' needs more often than my own?
- Am I scared that if I don't do as others ask they will leave me?
- If someone criticizes me, do I automatically believe their criticism to be true?
- Do I let other people define what my behavior means?
- When did I last say no to a person?
- What are 10 things I like to do with my time? Can I come up with a list quickly?
- What are the 10 things I hate doing? Am I even capable of strong feelings about things?

Benefits of setting strong and healthy boundaries

There are countless benefits to settings strong and healthy boundaries. While you can't expect to develop these overnight, if you're persistent in your assertiveness journey, you will be able to experience all the advantages of having your boundaries set and respected. Here's a list of what you can expect once you put in the hard work and learn how to stand your ground.

- You will feel more empowered
- You will be able to say 'no'
- You will be more in control of your life
- You will have healthier energy levels
- You will be able to clearly communicate your thoughts, needs, and desires
- You will feel more acknowledged, appreciated, and valued

- **You will attract supportive people**
- **You will speak up and feel heard**
- **You will develop a better awareness of your needs**
- **You will indulge in self-care without the guilt**
- **You will experience emotional balance and joy**
- **You will boost your self-esteem, self-image, and self-worth**
- **You will feel more courageous**
- **You will experience the freedom to be yourself**
- **You will honor your truth and values**

Now that you're aware of the common misconceptions around boundaries as well as the benefits of having strong and healthy limits, you can move on to start creating and enforcing the rules that will best suit your needs. In the next chapter, we thoroughly discuss the 10-step plan to establishing clear and consistent boundaries, in addition to how you can get other people in your life to respect your boundaries. We will also delve into more detail regarding boundary violations, how you should deal with difficult people who refuse to respect your protective barriers, and what to do with repeat offenders.

"Evaluating the benefits and drawbacks of any relationship is your responsibility. You do not have to passively accept what is brought to you. You can choose."

— Deborah Day

Chapter 3

Step 3: How to Respect Your Boundaries and Have Them Respected

In this chapter, we discuss the process of creating healthy boundaries that best serve your needs and meet your expectations. In addition to that, we will also tackle what may be the hardest part of the process, or by your standards, the most dreaded one, which is how to manage boundary violations when they occur and how to respond to the people responsible for these transgressions to ultimately get them to respect your boundaries.

How to establish healthy boundaries

Setting boundaries can be difficult, especially when you've lived all your life accommodating others to the point of neglecting yourself. While there is no one-size-fits-all when it comes to establishing these rules, there are however some guidelines you can follow to learn what works best for you in different contexts and with different people. Below are listed 10 comprehensive steps on how you can begin developing strong, clear, and consistent boundaries. So take the time to examine these measures to determine the best way to implement them in your life.

1.   Give yourself permission

If you haven't been able to successfully build healthy boundaries, then beneath the surface, you're probably convinced that you have 'no right ' to do so. This way of thinking has been so in-grained deep within your conscience that you simply cannot find a way to detach yourself from it.

Perhaps you don't see yourself worthy of the same respect, love, and appreciation you give to others around you. But the first step towards establishing healthy boundaries is to permit yourself to actually have those boundaries.

You can't expect others to recognize your efforts and show their gratitude to you if you're constantly sending the signal that you don't believe you deserve those things. Except you do, and so you need to be more mindful of the messages you send through your behavior and words.

The simplest example could be when someone apologizes and you say 'it's okay' instead of 'I accept your apology'. Saying 'it's okay' means you're fine with the wrong they've done and the distress they've caused. On the other hand, saying 'apology ac-cepted' means you recognize they've done something wrong and you choose to forgive them.

2.   Understand that your thoughts and feelings are equally important to others

Why are other people allowed to have boundaries but not you? Why must you feel less of a person and elevate other's thoughts, feelings, and needs above your own? Why are you so quick to idolize others and put them on a pedestal, yet you're incapable of giving even one ounce of that love and attention to yourself?

If you're serious about setting healthier boundaries, you need to realize that nobody's opinions, emotions, or desires are above those of anyone else. So you're not 'less important', valuable, or worthy than those around you. Your well-being is equally import-ant, your opinions just as valid, your thoughts just as valuable.

Anyone who tries to convince you otherwise is a person you must cut off from your life. There's enough negativity in your mind as it is, no need to pile up on that via other people's unsolicited malicious criticism.

Affirm your worth and value each day, remind yourself of your significance and purpose, repeat this phrase "I am worthy and my needs are important" until you believe it, and learn to disagree with those who make you think otherwise.

3.   Identify what you want and be specific about it

The main step in the process is to identify what you want. While this might seem like an obvious step to most, chances are, if you're used to taking care of others, meeting their needs, and making them happy, then you're so invested in them that you have no idea what it is that you really want. Since you've always been a giver more than a receiver, it could be a challenge to focus on your wants and desires over those of people in your life. With that said, you can make such a daunting task more manageable by starting small then gradually building your confidence. If you're struggling to come up with an answer, consider the following.

- **What values are important to you?**
- **What values do you want your friends, family members, or partner to have?**
- **What is the most important thing to you in your relationships?**
- **What bothers you the most in your relationships (whether it's friends, family, work, or other communities you're involved in)?**
- **What is something that you've always secretly wanted/ still want in life?**

Take the time to carefully craft your answers, as doing this will help you get the clarity you need on what's important to you and what matters the most.

4.   Delineate your boundaries

Before taking action, you need to be clear about your boundaries. Clear rules and limits will help you feel safer and more comfortable. So those fuzzy and ambiguous statements won't do simply because they won't be effective at all. Instead, you have to be very explicit and more straightforward with yourself. Be clear and concise, but avoid asking other people to change because that's just utter control and manipulation.

For instance, do you need your coworkers to stop bothering you with chat and gossip during work, or only when you have important projects to handle? Do you want your mother to stop dropping by or are you okay with that as long as she calls beforehand? Do you need your roommates to stop borrowing your clothes or is it just your favorite pieces that are off-limits?

Establishing clear 'no trespassing' lines will allow you to feel more confident about the things you expect in your space, in addition to reducing any misunderstandings or miscommunication with others. So take the time to identify the boundaries you want to be kept before you move onto implementing them in your daily life.

5.   Understand why you need those boundaries

Understanding why you need the boundaries you've set to be respected is your motivation to follow through with setting those boundaries. After all, if you don't have a compelling reason, why would you go out of your comfort zone and try to fix certain limits with others or yourself.

In addition to that, it's also important that you know why you're setting these rules in case someone attempts to talk you out of respecting those boundaries. You need to know how to defend the decisions you choose to take so you're prepared to do so if the occasion arises. Here are some examples to follow up with the questions mentioned in the previous point.

- **I don't want to be disturbed while working. If I can't focus on the important tasks at hand, I won't be able to complete my projects on time, and I don't want to let my team down.**
- **While I love my mother, I need her to stop dropping by**

whenever she feels the urge to. There are times when I'm not in a sociable mood and I need my own space. If she wants to visit, we can talk on the phone and schedule a date and time that works for both of us.

- **I need my roommate to understand that it's okay for her to borrow some of my clothes, but my favorite items are very special to me and only I can wear them.**

6.   Ask without apologizing

You're not doing anything wrong by setting and maintaining your boundaries, so there is no need to apologize for that. When you keep voicing how sorry you are for asking for one thing or the other, this only shows how guilty you feel about wanting to feel safe and comfortable in your own space.

In fact, one of the main reasons why people's boundaries weaken over time is due to the built-up guilt they feel each time they have to make a request. The goal here is being able to ask for what you want without feeling that guilt or the need to keep apologizing.

The first thing to do is to let go of all those long held beliefs that make you think asking for the things you want is selfish or greedy. Letting go of the things that don't serve you anymore is an important part of growth. Remember that you deserve to ask for what you want, in fact, it's your responsibility to set and enforce healthy boundaries.

7.   Don't set expectations

When setting boundaries, you need to be realistic about the things you want and how you can acquire them. This isn't meant to put you down or discourage you from pursuing your dreams. However, when you impose expectations that are too high, you're only setting yourself up for failure and disappointment.

For example, you can't expect someone to do something they've never done before just because you asked politely. Not only that but when you ask someone for something you want, you should do so without picturing the outcome you desire in your head.

In addition to that, if you expect someone else to handle your needs and desires, then you're only gonna be met with dissatisfaction and regret. Keep in mind that expectations are considered to be premeditated resentment when it comes to setting boundaries.

8.   Accept the answer if it's a no

You won't always get yes for an answer when you ask for something. While it might be nice to always get what you want, know that this is neither practical nor possible. The 'win' isn't in getting what you want per se, but it's more in the act of asking for it.

When it comes to putting healthy boundaries, the goal is to create a comfortable space where you or the other person are allowed to ask for the things you want, and not so much in getting a 'yes' straight away.

So if the other person says no, you need to respect their boundaries by accepting that answer. This is how you show your respect to others in a powerful way.

9.   Fulfill your own needs

If you ask your significant other, friend, or family member for something yet they find themselves unable to fulfill your needs, then you need to find a way to do it yourself. You shouldn't rely on others to accomplish the things you need to get done.

A little guidance and help when necessary is okay, but you shouldn't work on your tasks and projects only when nobody else can assist you in doing so. You have to learn that you're responsible for the choices you make and the decisions you follow through.

So you can't expect others to solve all of your problems just like they shouldn't expect you to solve theirs. Moreover, you have to be ready to accept the outcome of the boundaries you've set, regardless of how favorable or unfavorable it might be.

While there are times when you will successfully get what you want, there are other times when you won't. So it is detrimental that you learn to accept that end result no matter what it may be.

10.   Stop overcommitting

You're not particularly indebted to uphold every single commitment you've made (especially social obligations). You shouldn't try to please others at your own expense either. When you commit too much to other people and circumstances, this will only generate more anxiety and worries for you.

Not only that but in trying to keep up with all of your commitments, you will soon feel burned out and exhausted. This, in turn, will transform into resentment towards others due to how inconsiderate they are. But the thing is, you can't expect others to read your mind or know exactly how you feel about something.

Unless you make it clear from the get-go that you're comfortable with this and this and that but not with X, Y, and Z, then nobody will be able to 'sense' your pain or discomfort. Everyone is self-absorbed in the sense that we're all living inside our minds, we have our own worries, our own problems.

So trying to go out of one's own way to figure someone else out or gauge their level of happiness is a rare occurrence. Make a habit of voicing your thoughts and stop overcommitting. Learn to say no to non-essential things like get-togethers, work parties, or other events that aren't urgent.

How to get others to respect your boundaries

Establishing boundaries is no easy task, especially when you've been so used to focusing on others to the point of neglecting yourself. Of course, by now, you should be aware of your limits and what you're comfortable with. However, that doesn't make it any easier to communicate those ideas to others.

It's even harder when those around you have been habituated to you always going along with what they want, accepting their opinions as your own, and meeting their needs at all times. Now we get to the 'dreaded' part, that is, getting others to respect the boundaries you've fixed.

While there is no way to predict the outcome of this situation or how well your loved ones will take your newly established rules, you need to understand that those things are completely out of your control. You can't expect them to hold your boundaries for you either.

That's nobody's job but your own. In order for you to have your boundaries respected, you must actively protect them. There's no alternative to this. Picking the right people to hang around with won't absolve you of this responsibility either.

With that said, if you follow the guidelines below, you will have a much easier time not only getting others to respect your boundaries but earning the appreciation and recognition you deserve as well.

1.   Make your boundaries strong, consistent, and clear
This might sound redundant or obvious to you, but how can you expect others to know your boundaries if you're not clear and consistent about what you want? This only leads to confusion and sends the message that those 'rules' are mere suggestions rather than strong boundaries.

Sometimes, you may feel too tired to enforce those limits that you let something slide, allowing people to assume that you're okay with whatever is going on. So consistency is key in this case. While there's a lot of room for different rules and limits regarding all kinds of things, you need to know exactly what you're okay with, what you can tolerate, and what is simply off-limits.

If you're not sure whether it's okay with you to help a friend move apartments, how can you expect *them* to know whether it's okay with you? You don't necessarily have to figure these out according to each and every possible scenario, but it might help to think about your boundaries in a broader sense to get an insight ahead of time.

Here are some general areas to take into consideration.

- **Time:** this involves several things. For instance, think about how much time you're willing to spend with a specific person, whether it's on the phone, a get-together, or for the holidays. Once you've come to the conclusion of how much time you want to give to that person, it's time to find ways to enforce that boundary.

  Maybe you only call them when you have limited time, or maybe you let them know prior to meeting them that you're only available for one hour, etc. For added clarity, ask yourself "what do I say 'no' to when it comes to scheduling my time?".

- **Space:** perhaps you have a person in your life who doesn't respect your personal space and overstays their welcome. So you need to consider protecting your space by setting clear boundaries. Ask yourself: "how much do I allow them into my space?", "How close is too close?".

  Even allowing others to see your social media profiles can be categorized as personal space. In this context, protecting your space doesn't mean you hate that person. The same goes for unfriending or blocking them online.

  This is simply a way for you to be more selective about who can access what parts of your life. It's essential that you examine your space, determine what you're fine with sharing, and adjust your boundaries accordingly.

- **Energy:** this refers to how much emotional and mental energy you're willing to invest in the demands of other people. This, in particular, is a tricky boundary to establish due to how unstable and fluctuating our energy levels tend to be. To make it easier to assess, ask yourself: "how much energy do I have today to grant others?", and "how much energy do I want to give to this person based on their pattern of behavior?".

It's worth noting that it isn't only those difficult and abusive people that can drain your energy levels and kill your enthusiasm. In fact, sometimes it's also your close friends in need of emotional support when they're going through a hard time. So it's important that you remind yourself boundaries are essential, even with someone you love and hold dearly, especially if they're asking for more than what you can give.

2. Communicate your boundaries directly

While your boundaries won't necessarily adhere to a standard format that is applicable to everyone in your life, you still have a responsibility to make them clear and direct to the person involved. Sometimes, people are able to take the hint without you communicating your limits verbally. For example, if someone that you don't know all too well asks a personal question, and you reply with "why do you ask", they might read between the lines and drop the subject instantly, so you avoid a boundary violation without any conflict arising. On the other hand, if you find yourself storing anger and resentment toward people who don't seem to get the hint, then you're failing to communicate your boundaries. Keep in mind that it's your job to stand up for yourself. You can't expect other people to figure out what you want. So when in doubt, use these phrases to communicate your limits.

- **I'm not able to commit to that at the present moment**
- **I don't have that to offer right now**
- **I really appreciate you asking me, but I can't say yes to**

that
- **That's not going to work for me**
- **I don't feel comfortable doing that**
- **I'd rather not talk about it**
- **Please don't ask me about that again, I already told you not to last time you asked**
- **My answer is no for now, but I will let you know if something changes**

3. Don't let boundary violations slide

This is the toughest part of the process, but you need to understand that nobody is responsible for defending your boundaries but yourself. So when these are crossed, you need to be prepared to take action.

For example, if you tell someone you will meet them at 5 pm at the coffee shop with a 15-minute window of give or take, and they're 30 minutes late but you waited for them anyway, then you've failed to react to a limit-crossing.

If they had no valid reason, by your terms, as to why they were late, then you can't just say 'they should know better' or yell at them for being late. You're the one who set that 15-minute waiting boundary, so you should be the one to protect it. If you think that amount of time is too low or unrealistic, then don't set it as a limit in the first place.

Only establish rules and limits you're willing to enforce and follow through. While you can't predict how others will respond to the boundaries you create, you can, however, decide the course of action following any violation that occurs.

For instance, if you lend your friend some money and you give them a week to pay you back, then they don't pay you back within that time frame, but you still lend them money again regardless, then you've failed to protect your boundaries.

How to respond to people who violate your boundaries

Resenting others for crossing your boundaries is often the result of helplessness. However, cutting those people off, while sometimes necessary, is commonly done in a premature way, simply because of the misconception that there are no other options.

Breaking free from other people won't help you improve on protecting your boundaries, so you need to ensure you've done your part before giving up on the people in your life. You're not entirely helpless when it comes to facing boundary violations.

Though you were defenseless as a child if someone violated your rules and limits, you're an adult now, and you have several options and recourses at your disposal. You're responsible for defending your borders and keeping the people who cross them accountable for their actions.

This point raises two pertinent questions: "should I keep someone in my life, even if they don't respect my boundaries?", and "when should I consider cutting a toxic person out of my life?". In this part, we discuss the best ways to respond to boundary violations and how you can deal with difficult people who are reluctant to respect your boundaries.

1.   Decide whether this boundary is negotiable
Some of your boundaries might be more vital to your well-being than others, but how do you identify which ones are essential and which ones are more flexible? The first step in this process is to distinguish what you're willing to accept from what you see as intolerable or non-negotiable. If there's something you can compromise for the sake of a new relationship and its integrity then that shows you where to push the line.

Compromise can be a good thing, as long as it doesn't harm you personally, or make you fall back to old habits of people-pleasing. So you need to be aware that compromise does not indicate abandoning your needs to satisfy someone else, nor accepting treatment that you normally consider to be a deal-breaker.

If a person in your life repeatedly violates your boundaries, you can't keep accepting that behavior and sit back while you wait for them to change, because chances are, they never will. Instead, you need to make an assertive decision of what you can let slide and what you won't allow in your life.

2.   Record the boundary violations

When a person continues to cross your boundaries, again and again, it's time to gather information. You can use a journal to document the nature of this disrespect in juxtaposition with your thoughts, feelings, and emotions. In addition to that, you should also take note of how you responded to these violations, and what you think you should have said instead.

This will not only help you keep track of how often violations occur but also give you some insight on how you handle these situations. Are you not being clear enough or assertive enough? Do your boundaries have weak spots? Are they inconsistent? Do you tend to react in anger and frustration leading to more conflict down the line?

This practice will help you learn more about yourself as well as the boundary offenders. For instance, you might notice that you're not being consistent with setting healthy boundaries, which could be the potential trigger to these violations. Whatever you find out, make adjustments accordingly so everyone around you is clear on what your limits are and know when not to cross them.

3.   Accept that not everyone will respect your boundaries

While you'd like to be able to convince others to respect your boundaries, sadly, that plainly isn't the truth. There are people who aren't willing to listen to others, who never take others seriously, and who keep overstepping boundaries time and time again. Although it comes as a shock or disappointment, you just can't expect to change others simply because you're showing them love, compassion, and kindness.

You can't expect them to 'return the favor' and treat you with the same respect you have for them. In these instances, you must choose not to invest your energy and time into correcting their behavior.

You have no control over their minds, so instead of getting wrapped up in getting them to let go of their toxic attitude, focus on why they're behaving the way they are and how you can best respond to their recurring transgressions.

While it will take a lot of energy and willpower not to give in to their provocations, you have to maintain a positive mindset and actively choose not to give them the satisfaction of engagement. This can lead to a tremendous power shift as your lack of reaction will make the process of provoking you less 'fun' for them.

Often, this can cause the boundary violations to stop. Do note, however, that this is not the same as physical abuse, as that will require authority intervention, and in that case, you need to speak to someone, lodge a formal complaint, or contact the police.

4.   Practice loving detachment

When dealing with a repeat boundary offender, sometimes you can get too frustrated because of the lack of control you feel. However, instead of beating yourself up for not being able to convince them or make them respect your limits, perhaps it's time to disengage.

The best thing you can do when you feel like you've hit a wall or an impenetrable impasse is to detach yourself from the situation. Arguing will lead nowhere and trying to manipulate the outcome to align with what you want will only leave you feeling helpless and defeated.

So accept that you simply can't control other people's behavior and remove yourself from the situation instead. You can do this by:

- **Not participating in unproductive conversations**
- **Declining invitations that entail spending time with them**
- **Choosing not to react to their disrespectful behavior**
- **Hanging up the phone**
- **Physically leaving an uncomfortable or harmful situation**
- **Responding in a different way (i.e: shrugging off a rude remark or making a joke of it to shift the dynamic of the interaction)**
- **Letting them make their own decision and face the outcome of that decision**
- **Taking space away from an argument**
- **Not offering unsolicited advice**

5.   Consider limiting contact or cutting them off

So what do you do when you've established your boundaries and you're actively working on enforcing them, yet certain people in your life still choose to ignore them completely? Should you even allow someone to stay in your life if they don't respect your limits? This question is subjective because it solely depends on your particular situation, meaning it's up to you to decide who stays and who leaves.

While you can coexist with people who show no respect for your boundaries and continuously walk all over them, this wouldn't be possible without strong, consistent, and vigilant boundary-setting. It's important to be aware that it is your right to remove yourself from the relationships you find to be too toxic.

Granted, some contexts are harder to detach yourself from than others. For instance, it's no easy feat to disengage from the 'permanent fixtures' in your life, namely your close family members, parents, siblings, and in-laws, compared to difficult friends, roommates, or coworkers. However, you still have the option of detaching yourself from these people using many degrees of distancing and estrangement.

On the other hand, cutting off people completely can often prove to be the only viable solution in handling certain individuals in your life. One point you need to pay close attention to is how emotionally and mentally taxing it feels to remain in contact with a particular person.

If you find that you're very preoccupied with their pattern of behavior and often fantasize about setting strict boundaries or getting into a series of arguments with this person, then this emotional and mental absorption can be a big hint that you've reached the point of saturation and so more drastic measures need to be taken.

The Takeaway

Now you might be thinking 'this information is great and all, but when I'm in the moment, all of my intentions to set and enforce my boundaries go right out the window". This mindset is more common than you think. Struggling with maintaining your boundaries can happen for a number of reasons.

It could be because that person is abusive and in that given situation, you're too overwhelmed to stand your ground. Or maybe you tell yourself 'it's okay to let it slide this time', but later on realize that you shouldn't have done that. No matter how complex a reason it is, you need to ground yourself at that moment and try to remember why setting this boundary is important to you in the first place.

Is it because you want to be more independent, more fulfilled, and less hurt or emotionally scarred? Is it because you want to protect your family? In addition to that, you also need to think of the consequences your lax boundaries might have.

Asking yourself "based on the pattern of behavior of this person, what is likely to happen if I loosen my boundaries with them?" can be tremendously helpful in these situations. So if you find that you're unable to keep yourself accountable for enforcing your limits, enlisting somebody else's help can be beneficial.

The support of a dear friend or loved one can be necessary sometimes, especially when you're too exhausted that you begin to consider giving in to that toxic person's demands. Just remember that boundaries are not set in stone, that they're flexible, and you can always readjust them to fit your needs as you grow and change.

"No" is a complete sentence."

— Annie Lamott

Chapter 4

Step 4: When the Word "No" Leaves You Feeling Guilty

It's a simple word, isn't it? Short, concise, straight to the point. No. One syllable. So why is it so hard to say, to utter those two letters? Why is it that we keep dancing around, coming up with elaborate justifications to sugarcoat our intentions? Why do we keep apologizing for not being able to engage in emotionally and mentally taxing activities and ventures?

Why do we feel the crushing weight of guilt the minute we're asked to do something we're not comfortable with? Why do we go out of our way to say 'yes' and give in to the requests of others at the expense of our own well-being when a simple word would have granted us our freedom and happiness?

Perhaps it's because of how much power that 'no' holds, how much assertiveness, how much intensity and vehemence. And like any powerful instrument, this word can either liberate us from our shackles or wound us like a soldier falling on his own sword. As much as we hate rejection, we also hate reject*ing*, maybe even to a greater extent.

Consider the power and authority you wield simply by saying 'no'. This word can your ticket out of that brunch date you're dreading. It can prevent others from taking up so much of your time. It can send the signal to someone who keeps taking advantage of your kindness that it's time to stop. It can save you money, effort, and energy.

The word 'no' is a fundamental instrument that allows you to pre-serve your resources for the things that matter to you the most.

Though perhaps because it's so powerful it could also be counter-intuitive or even dangerous at times.

Every time you say the word no to decline someone else's demand or invitation, unpleasantness and conflict might arise. It might come as a disappointment to the people you hold dear, hurt their feelings, or make them angry and sullen. Then the moment you pronounce that word, you're suddenly hit with a crashing wave of guilt and remorse...

"Uh-Oh, her expression changed, now she looks really sad and disappointed, if I agreed then everything would have been fine", "I might have offended him, if only I said yes", "I shouldn't have declined her invitation, I was going to spend the evening at home by myself anyway", "I really had no reason for not attending her party" ...

If you're used to taking on more responsibility in your relationships with others, then you probably have a hard time saying no. You always assume it's your job to keep everyone around you happy and fulfilled. So you go out of your way to accommodate their needs even when your plate is over brimming.

Why you need to say no

While there's nothing wrong with being kind, thoughtful, and accommodating, the issue arises when you're constantly agreeing to things, making engagements, and committing to tasks that not only please everyone but yourself, but also for which you have absolutely no time, nor willingness.

Your close friends and family members deserve your love and emotional support but they're not entitled to all of your time and energy. And although you do have to work for a living, you shouldn't stand for being exploited and undervalued.

From the moment you wake up until you go to bed, you're continuously bombarded with requests, demands, and invitations. Things that provoke an irrepressible urge to scream "I don't want to" or "Leave me alone!". Things that incite a thunderous desire to say no...

Yet more often than not, you find yourself summoning up a smile and agreeing to everything. So out of guilt and disinclination to confrontation, you take on more and more things, you overcommit, you make more and more engagements until you're drowning under the pressure of having to meet everyone else's expectations.

You agree to attend events you know you will hate, parties full of people who drain you emotionally. One time it's helping a friend move all the junk they own from one city to another, then another time it's going to some multilevel marketing meeting that your neighbor is hosting which you have no interest in whatsoever, or it's painting furniture for an entire afternoon with your berating brother. So you invest your time and energy in other people's priorities until you're too exhausted to take care of yourself and your needs.

Accepting a dear friend's request or invitation is great if you enjoy spending time with them or you can afford to provide them with what they need. What isn't so great, however, is when you resent that person and find them too disagreeable to hang out with, or when fulfilling their demand will cause you tremendous stress and discomfort.

This process will only deplete your resources, whether it be money, time, and energy, on things that don't matter at all or that aren't necessarily important to you. So each time you say 'yes' when you really want to say 'no', you're wasting a little more of those resources.

You can say 'no' and still be nice

You have to understand that when you say 'no' to someone, that's not the end of the world for them, in the same way it isn't for you when you're faced with rejection. For instance, let's say you have to attend a work event, your babysitter canceled on you last minute, and you need someone to babysit, so you ask your neighbor. Now your neighbor also happens to have some other commitment and so is unavailable.

You hear the word 'no', you don't suddenly act in disdain, get angry at her, or lash out. You accept the 'no' reasonably and you move on to explore other options. Well, it's very much the same scenario for others as well. Unless you're dealing with a toxic or difficult person, chances are, they will accept the 'no' and move on to explore other options too. Even if the other person gets angry or disappointed, their reactions are their own, which means they're out of your control.

The issue is when they keep asking, again and again. That's when you must not give in. Even if they think they will wear you down eventually, just keep giving the same answer over again. Don't soften up and start with a 'maybe' that leads to an 'alright, I'll do it". Like we've established previously when you're inconsistent with the boundaries you set, that sends the wrong message to those around you and signals to them that you're not serious about your limits or that those rules are mere suggestions.

7 effective ways to say 'no' without feeling guilty

Saying 'no' isn't rude or disrespectful, you can say no and still be nice. It won't suddenly turn you into a heartless monster or a cruel and ungrateful beast either. Saying 'no' with sensitivity and compassion is a skill and like all skills, practice makes perfect. Below are 4 effective ways to say 'no' without feeling guilty.

1.   Offer an alternative

This is probably the easiest way to say 'no'. Start by declining the request but, as a consolation prize, follow up with an alternative. "I have a previous engagement at that time so I can't go antique shopping with you, but I believe X will definitely be up to the task" or "My schedule doesn't allow me to attend your charity event but I would love to make a donation". Whatever the situation is, make sure you're not giving a 'counteroffer' just because you want to feel less guilty for dismissing their request. The objective here is to be helpful, and not to lessen the remorse.

2.   Put the blame elsewhere

While you don't have to offer any justifications for declining an offer or request, if you don't feel you've reached that level of assertiveness yet, you can always blame your inability to meet a person's demands on something else, whether it be objective or subjective. You could say you have a busy schedule, a heavy workload, or an appointment that you simply can't miss. If you want to avoid the awkwardness of "You're busy this Friday, how about next Friday?", then add a simple "I'll let you know if anything changes" at the end.

3.   Turn it into a compliment

Instead of outright rejection, you can say no and tie it with a compliment. For instance, "Thank you for thinking of me that's very nice of you", or "You're very thoughtful for asking me first, I appreciate it". Show the other person empathy or give them words of encouragement while still standing your ground. Convey your good nature and make them feel good by communicating that you hear them and you truly understand their situation even if you ultimately can't accept or agree.

4.   Say no without apologizing

Understand that, similar to guilt, apologizing is aimed to redeem yourself for when you've done something wrong, and not for a simple 'no' because you can't take on more things. Declining someone's request can be done politely and graciously and the other person won't even miss the "I'm sorry". For example, "what a great idea to knit special scarves for the book club this month! Though I have to admit, I'm not the person for the job. But I can bake a mean apple pie". Swift, clear, and polite. No apologies necessary!

The Takeaway

When you feel inclined to reject someone's demand, remember these 4 strategies and work on implementing them in your day-to-day life. While it might take some trial and error to learn how to better stick to your guns, ultimately, saying 'no' will liberate you from the commitments and engagements that don't serve you, so you have more time to do what you love.

Chapter 5

Step 5: People-pleasing at the Expense of Your Own Happiness

There's nothing wrong in showing kindness and support to the people in your life, even pushing the envelope from time to time and doing them a favor that you're not too thrilled about solely because you care about them and their well-being. However, when you start setting their priorities above yours and you begin to agree to their every request or demand in spite of it being at the expense of your own happiness, then that when you know you've reached the point of people-pleasing.

For many, this resounding desire and eagerness to please or comply stems from self-esteem issues and the need to feel liked and accepted. On the other hand, this habit can also develop after an extensive history of maltreatment. So in this case, an individual will decide that their only hope for better treatment is to try and please the people who mistreated them to keep them happy and content.

People-pleasing starts to become a problem the moment you choose to allow the wants and desires of those around you to have more importance than your own needs. This not only authorizes others to take advantage of you, but it can also cause you a great deal of stress, burnout, as well as intense feelings of resentment and anger.

In this chapter, we discuss the telltale signs that you're a people-pleaser, how this bad habit can affect your life, as well as how you can overcome this vicious pattern.

5 Signs you're a people-pleaser

People-pleasing can be extremely damaging to you as well as your relationships, not to mention how mentally taxing it can prove to be. Here are 5 signs that you show you may be too adamant to please everyone around you.

1.   You're quick to agree with everyone

While being a good listener is a great social skill to have, you can't pretend to agree with everything the other person says just because you want to be like or for fear of offending them. If you keep going along with ideas and opinions you don't agree with just to keep people happy or win their approval and validation, you will inevitably find yourself engaging in behavior that completely contradicts your values, so you're only setting yourself up for frustration and self-loathing.

2.   You feel responsible for how others feel

Taking the time to acknowledge and think about how the way you act affects others is a good thing. With that said, being convinced that you're responsible for other people's happiness, satisfaction, and well-being is a very unhealthy mindset. Each person is in charge of their own emotions, feelings, and thoughts, so you can't expect to influence something that is beyond your control. Not only is it exhausting to keep up with the wants and needs of everyone around you, but it also leaves you very little time and energy to take care of your own. Making unnecessary sacrifices will only lead to martyrdom and disappointment since you will always expect others to reciprocate your behavior.

3.   You apologize even when you're not to blame

A massive indicative sign that you're a people-pleaser is how ready you are to take the blame and apologize even when you're not at fault. You're constantly saying you're sorry as you excessively blame yourself or fear that people around you are also blaming you. Frequent apologies, especially when uncalled for, can be a sign of a much bigger problem. With that said, try to remember that you don't need to apologize for being you.

4.   You have a hard time saying no

More often than not, you find yourself agreeing to other people's requests even when you don't feel inclined to do so simply because it's easier than saying 'no'. While many people agree to do things they're not particularly very fond of, a recurrent pattern of this can be an issue since it shows other people that their needs are above yours. So as a consequence, those individuals will begin to ignore your boundaries and keep asking for more because they know you will do it regardless.

5.   You can't stand the thought of someone being annoyed
with you

People-pleasing is a habit that is mainly centered on the fear of other people's anger and possible retaliation. So even if that person is not necessarily mad at or frustrated with you, you still feel as if you've failed at pleasing them and keeping them happy. You might rush to say sorry or try everything you can think of to bring them comfort. What is dangerous in this situation is that your inability to bear others being displeased with you can cause you to compromise your values. This will only lead to further frustration and feelings of inadequacy when the reality you're living completely contradicts your true self or reflects it poorly.

How people-pleasing can affect your life

People-pleasing is not inherently bad, considering how part of building meaningful relationships with others involves taking their wants, needs, and emotions into account. Doing this often comes from a place of love, affection, or concern.

However, when you're constantly seeking the validation and approval of others, this usually means that you're neglecting your own feelings and priorities. So you do what you think other people want or need to like you.

You start putting on an act and pretending you enjoy all the things they enjoy. You show your eagerness to please, your enthusiasm to help, despite how differently you might feel deep within. This is not only an honest way to live, as you constantly exist in a state of inner/outer conflict, but being a compulsive people-pleaser can hurt you as well as your relationships.

The more people take advantage of you, the more resentful and frustrated you feel. And because you're so used to giving your all, you also expect others to reciprocate, which means your relationships will never be satisfying or fulfilling enough simply because the high standards you've set aren't been met.

In addition to that, there's also the increased stress you have to deal with and high chances of burnout. Not only do you not have the time to invest in things you enjoy, but you also get less time to do the things you really need to do.

So to get the essentials done, you sacrifice sleep or work long hours to compensate, eventually falling prey to exhaustion, sleep deprivation, worry, and stress. This can also ruin your relationship with your partner when they start asking why you agree with everyone or why you keep apologizing for things you had nothing to do with.

How to overcome the pattern of people-pleasing

If you want to break the pattern and let go of the bad habit of people-pleasing, examining the circumstances in which this behavior shows up is a great first step to take. So building your awareness around the situations in which you have a penchant for people-pleasing will allow you to start making positive changes and take back control of your own happiness. Here are some ways you can start doing that.

1.   Practice putting yourself first

If you genuinely enjoy helping others and offering your compassion and emotional support, you need to realize that you can't do that in good spirits unless you start to take care of yourself. You want the love you express to others to be genuine, and that wouldn't be possible if you're secretly resenting or dreading completing the task at hand. If you're angry, frustrated, and distressed, you're in no place to give others what you cannot give even an ounce of to yourself.

2.   Reinforce your boundaries

Developing healthy boundaries is the ultimate way to learn how to say 'no' and stop being a people-pleaser. So next time someone asks for help or you feel compelled to intervene, take a moment, and ask yourself how you feel about that action. Then think about whether you actually have time to take care of your needs first.

Will you have to sacrifice your limited free time or will you be skipping out on a priority? Now think about how helping that person will make you feel. Will you enjoy helping them or will you be resentful? Answering these questions before you give a definite answer will make it easier for you to reinforce your boundaries where needed.

3.   Wait until you're explicitly asked for help

No matter how tempting it might be to jump in with a solution, suggestion, or an offer to help, try to challenge yourself to wait until you're explicitly asked for help. If your friend goes off on a rant about her roommate and how insufferable she's being, instead of listing off pieces of advice or tips, try to genuinely listen to her complaints. She might not be looking for ways to deal with the situation but rather for emotional support, empathy, and validation.

4.   Understand the importance of being authentic

Instead of always agreeing with others or doing what they want, try to be more honest and truer to yourself. There's immense value in authenticity that you've been missing out on. Understand that everyone is unique in their own way and that having a different opinion than that of a friend doesn't mean you're suddenly sworn enemies. You can disagree and still coexist in the same environment. So learn to listen to yourself, act authentically, and connect with who you are and what you value.

5.   Embrace self-acceptance

The journey to self-acceptance can be long and strenuous, but like any other odyssey, this process is ever-changing and continuously evolving. With that said, it's up to you to put those wheels in motion and propel yourself toward growth and self-love. Once you start to value yourself and become more aware of your worth, you will be able to become more assertive in your choices and this newfound confidence will help you better navigate day-to-day life.

The Takeaway

It's never too late to start living a free life, a life of your own choosing, one that isn't dependent of those around you and how they feel. Once you get a hang of the 5 practices mentioned above, you can finally lead a lifestyle on your own terms, one that honors your values and speaks to your authentic self. While the path towards full self-acceptance might be arduous, it can be just as rewarding when you finally break free from that people-pleasing mindset.

"Because children take everything personally, they believe that if they are being mistreated, it's because they haven't been "good enough." Being good as an adult makes them believe, incorrectly, that they have some control in life. They think that they will be rewarded for their goodness and that it will protect them from harm."

— Marcia Sirota

Chapter 6

Step 6: Codependency-Saving Others Over Myself

As human beings, we have an inherent desire and inclination to connect with each other and form strong long-lasting bonds. There are countless instances throughout the course of history where our survival has been intrinsically linked to our ability to build and nurture healthy and secure relationships.

Decades of research in human behavior show that communication is a major aspect of creating and maintaining those bonds. As we all know, there are several types of communication, some more effective and powerful than others.

While there is no magic formula to ensure that you're conveying an accurate expression of your thoughts, opinions, and feelings, there are, however, specific skills that you can develop to build healthier relationships.

In this chapter, we focus more on what *not* to do when it comes to relationships, and what can completely throw off a relationship so it ends up at the negative side of the spectrum, and that is codependency.

Read along to learn more about what codependency is, the indicative signs that you're codependent, as well as how to break this cycle and practice creating healthier connections with others.

What is Codependency

Codependency is one of those clinical terms that often tends to get overused or casually tossed around. This makes it a bit harder to define because of how frequently it's detached from its true context. So what is codependency ... really?

While it's part of our human nature to rely on one another for help and support, this verges on the unhealthy side when we begin to depend on that person to make us feel important, valuable, and that we matter.

Rather than choosing to depend on the other person for certain things or genuinely enjoying what they can offer us, codependent relationships are deeply rooted in desperation and compulsiveness.

So much so that in extreme cases, the person will go as far as to build their entire identity around caring for their partner, children, friends, or family members. When that relationship becomes majorly one-sided, an imbalance occurs in the dynamic, with one person desiring embedded codependency and the other looking for diffuse independence.

4 Signs You're Codependent

1.   You fear the other person will abandon you
Feeling sad about the idea of your partner or friend, whom you have a codependent relationship with, leaving is completely normal. On the other hand, experiencing frequent, unprovoked, and sometimes even irrational fear and anxiety about this is a definite sign of codependency.

So to remedy this fear of abandonment, you try to make yourself useful and needed by obsessively taking care of the other person and making them your responsibility. You believe that as long as the other person needs you, then they won't leave and abandon you. It's pretty much a lousy insurance policy that you take out on abandonment.

2.   Your self-esteem is built on the other person's opinion
Codependent relationships experience a wide fluctuation in self-esteem and confidence. In attaching yourself to the other person to an unhealthy level, you start to build your self-esteem around their emotions, feelings, and opinions.

So much so that any minor dip in the display of love and affection, even over very short periods of time, can tank your self-esteem to the lowest levels. Unfortunately, in many cases, no matter how much attention you receive, it will never be enough.

3.   You're constantly excusing bad behavior
When you're too defensive of the other person, and you constantly feel the urge to excuse their poor judgment and bad behavior, this is another sign that you might be in a codependent relationship.

This can spiral into so much toxicity that you start to feel responsible for the other person's actions to the point of coming to their defense or apologizing on their behalf despite the atrocities they've committed.

4.   You have very demanding expectations of the other person
Because of your reliance on the other person to feel valuable, important, and good about yourself, you might be unconsciously setting very high expectations for them to meet. You might also be outrageously demanding of their time and energy.

So when the other person takes some time for themselves, you could see it as a lack of affection or proof of indifference, when in reality their feelings for you are unchanged. Accordingly, you will constantly look for validation and reinforcement of their love for you.

Tips to Break the Cycle of Codependency

1. Take the time to get to know yourself

A key step to take when attempting to break the cycle of codependency is getting to know yourself better. Figure out who you are, what you like, and what your purpose is outside of your relationships.

When you become more aware of what defines you as a person as well as your passions and dreams, you learn to be more content with yourself, which, in turn, will help boost your confidence, reducing codependent feelings and behavior.

2. Step out of your comfort zone

A great way to overcome the burden of codependency is to venture out into the world and learn to do things on your own. So step out of your comfort zone, embrace new experiences, strengthen friendships, take up new activities, and do things that challenge you, or make you feel uncomfortable. This is how you learn to 'survive' without others and find value in being truly yourself and *with* yourself in the present moment.

3. Examine your personal needs and their importance

Putting the needs of others above your own is partly what fuels your codependency. This is why it's important to reassess your relationships with other people in order for you to identify your personal needs.

When you begin to recognize the things you need to do to take better care of yourself, this plays a major role in overcoming the vicious cycle of codependency.

Subsequently, having a better understanding of your needs means you're able to tell when they're being met and when they aren't. If not, then you need to rethink your priorities to make sure you're fulfilled and content.

The Takeaway

Codependency is more common among relationships than you think. So if you identified with the telling signs, don't beat yourself up about it. However, it's important to build awareness around the detrimental effects it can have on your life. While breaking the cycle isn't all too easy, it's well worth the energy and effort to secure your happiness in the long run.

"Many of us live in denial of who we truly are because we fear losing someone or something-and there are times that if we don't rock the boat, too often the one we lose is ourselves...It feels good to be accepted, loved, and approved of by others, but often the membership fee to belong to that club is far too high of a price to pay."

— Dennis Merritt Jones

Chapter 7

Step 7: Learning to Separate Your Stuff from Other People's Stuff

Attachment can be defined as a feeling that connects and binds one person to another person, to an object, to a cause, or to an ideal. There are three main styles of attachment, and those are secure attachments, anxious attachments, and avoidant attachments. Now each style affects us differently, from our choice of the people we surround ourselves with to how these relationships unfold and progress over time.

- **Secure attachment:** being comfortable with intimacy; better satisfaction in relationships; leading a life independent from others; allowing others to lead their lives independently as well; better understanding of when to be honest and supportive; reasonable reaction in face of conflict; adequate self-esteem levels.

- **Anxious attachment:** feeling unworthy in relationships with others; taking everything personally; demanding expectations; defining oneself through one's relationships; codependency; self-sabotage; fear of being alone; extreme clinginess and neediness; desperate acts to get the other person's attention; low self-esteem.

- **Avoidant attachment:** complete avoidance of relationships; distancing oneself from others; sabotaging relationships out of fear of abandonment; emotional distancing; feelings of overwhelm and mood swings; fear of being hurt; unclear ideas of getting one's needs met by others.

While these attachment styles -secure, anxious, and avoidant- have mainly been studied in the relationship between children and their caregivers, they do continue well into adolescence and adulthood, and not only in romantic relationships.

The truth is, we tend to take our attachment style everywhere with us, whether it be in the workplace, friendships, family relationships, or other networks. Since we only know one particular way of getting our emotional needs met, we tend to put it to practice in all of our endeavors.

It's very possible that you can spend your entire life not knowing there are other styles of attachment, healthier ones. So you go about expecting everyone else to do relationships the same way you do.

This not only sets unrealistic standards for others, since whatever they do will never be sufficient or come close to the level of sacrifice you've established, but it also sets you up for future frustration and even resentment. It's only when this way of forming bonds and progressing in relationships starts to hurt you and cause you tremendous pain that you take a step back and rethink your attachment pattern.

While the process of self-reflection can elicit difficult emotions and bring back painful experiences to the surface, the insight you gain will allow you to get a clearer understanding of yourself outside of those relationships, so ultimately you can start to separate your own stuff from other people's stuff.

How to Separate Your Stuff from Other People's stuff

Keep in mind that there are no 'bad' or 'good' attachment styles, you simply need to identify the pattern you most relate to and move on to improve the aspects of communication where there's room for growth and learning.

Most importantly, you need to understand that these styles are not set in stone, and while they tend to be lasting, they're also flexible and capable of evolving. You can develop a secure attachment style if you put in the work and practice some of the strategies discussed in this book.

Below, we list a few pointers on how you can begin to challenge the fears and insecurities that have been instilled and enabled by your attachment style so you can ultimately learn to exist on your own and stop taking responsibility for other people's thoughts, feelings, and emotions.

Shift the focus to yourself

Through your attachment to others, you tend to put other people at the center of your mental and emotional world. Detaching and separating yourself from others means you need to shift the focus to yourself. This doesn't entail a permanent detachment from others, but rather a proactive one that you practice whenever you notice you're getting too wrapped up inside that person's life that you start thinking for them and acting on their behalf. Take your attention away from that person and redirect it to yourself by asking yourself "How am I doing?" or "What can I do for myself right now?".

Define where you end and where others begin

When you're used to associating your happiness with that of those around you, it can be hard to define where you end and where others begin. So much so that their anger becomes yours, the same way their sadness or satisfaction does.

It's important that you identify what you're carrying that isn't yours. When you delineate the limits for each person in your life, you will discover that in many instances you were acting out other people's feelings instead of your own.

So ask yourself what behaviors you have that aren't in alignment with who you are. Then think about what you do, whether intentionally or unintentionally, that blocks the love you'd like to give to yourself. Once you pinpoint what doesn't belong to you, it's time to give it back!

Hold responsibility only for yourself

When evaluating your needs, you might be tempted to bend your boundaries for someone you've once let in, who seems reluctant to be left out. When asking for what you need, you might feel the impulse to soothe the other person and retract because of their defensive reaction.

When taking time for yourself, you might feel guilty to the point of overcompensating others for what you think is a luxury you shouldn't have allowed yourself to indulge in.

However, no matter how tempting it might be and no matter how familiar it might seem, never hold responsibility for other people's reactions or feelings. You're only responsible for who you are, so it's time you let go of the control you've been pursuing and release all of the unhealthy behavior that's brought you to where you are today.

The Takeaway

Understand that you are responsible for your stuff and your stuff only. Everyone else is responsible for theirs. Contrary to your beliefs, you're not helping nor showing support to anyone by trying to control their emotions. While asking for what you need isn't always easy, if you're truly committed to making a positive change in your life, then you have to do it. The more practice you have in this regard, the more you'll be able to determine what's yours, what belongs to others, and how you can draw the line between the two.

*"Success and failure come and go, but don't let them define you.
It's who you are that matters."*

— Kamal Ravikant

Chapter 8

Step 8: Standing in Your Truth and Honoring Your Authenticity

"Live your truth". You've probably heard this phrase all too often, perhaps from your health crazed friend who is obsessed with wellness and clean eating, or your newly converted green smoothie addict coworker who won't shut up about their hot yoga classes.

But beneath the secret judgment you hold, and maybe even the condescendence, have you ever stopped to consider what that phrase really means? It's a simple statement, isn't it? Yet it holds so much meaning, so much power.

Perhaps you've been quick to dismiss it because it makes no sense to you. Living your truth, what does that even mean? It seems too obvious of a phrase that you never took a chance to dig deeper and read between the lines.

Are you even aware of your truth? You might think "well, I am honest, most of the time, and I try to speak my mind whenever I can, so what else is there to it, really?". Standing in your truth is not a practice, it's not something you suddenly decide to take up.

It requires a lot of time and effort on your part. Living your truth simply means living your values, living with integrity, being authentic to who you are in all your endeavors, being honest, not only to other people but most importantly to yourself, it's talking the talk but also walking the walk.

Most of us spend our lives trying to live up to expectations and definitions. In this way, we're straying from who we really are because we're living to be a different version from our true selves.

In this chapter, we talk about uncovering your truth and how standing in your truth and honoring your authenticity will free you from the shackles of your past and set you on the path to a life full of joy, inspiration, fulfillment, and energy.

Uncovering Your Truth

While there is no magic solution or quick fix to the process of uncovering your truth, there are, however, a few steps you can follow to unearth the best version of yourself and the most authentic one.

In a world filled with engagements, commitments, and never-ending distractions, it's hard to take the time for self-reflection, when you're constantly chasing one thing or the other. Especially considering the endless profusion of messages about who and what you should aim to be.

We're continuously bombarded with ideals of beauty, intelligence, humor, and confidence that we tend to lose ourselves while trying to decipher these signals and how to emulate them. So how do you regain focus and redirect your energy to the things that matter to you rather than what 'should be' by someone else's standards?

The best way to go about this is to conduct a personal inventory. This process requires utter focus and a serene environment that incites self-reflection. So take the time to breathe and think about these questions.

- **What are your core values?**
- **What do you stand for?**
- **What are your strengths and weaknesses?**

- **What self-limiting beliefs are stopping you from unlocking your potential?**
- **What boundaries are the most important to you?**
- **Do you take the time and effort to honor those boundaries?**
- **What is your mission in life?**
- **What makes you happy? How can you have more of this?**
- **What are your passions, or things that you secretly long for?**
- **What drives you to be the best version of yourself?**

Identifying, understanding, and eventually living your truth is one of the most important things you will ever do in life, so you need to make it count.

How Standing in Your Truth Will Free You

Standing in your truth isn't about drastically changing who you are or 'fixing' the damaged parts of yourself. On the contrary, it's all about self-acceptance and finding happiness from within. When you start honoring your authenticity, you're gradually becoming the strong and confident person you were meant to be.

Living with integrity through actions and communications with yourself as well as those around you will liberate you, not only from the fears that have always held you back but also from seeking the validation of others. You're simply unleashing your full potential to become more comfortable with who you are through the process of self-actualization.

This also means you'll be better prepared to deal with adversity as having a strong sense of self will empower you and provide you with an anchor to ground you when you're facing bumps along the road or challenging situations. Your newfound balanced outlook will help you manage unexpected detours and provide you with the confidence in knowing no matter what happens you will be okay.

In addition to that, when you are anchored in your truth, you have a more accurate compass to help you navigate life all while setting healthy boundaries and taking better care of yourself without feeling guilty.

This is essential in today's society, as we're constantly met with a barrage of ideas driving the message that women should feel guilty when they take time for themselves.

Hence the expressions "treat yourself", "splurge", or "indulge". But standing in your truth will prevent you from being derailed or influenced by these external directives that encourage you to overlook your own well-being.

The Takeaway

Standing in your truth is an essential part of your journey towards living a more authentic and fulfilling life. You've tried going along with everyone else's feelings, you've tried agreeing with everything they say, you've tried accommodating them and even enabling their bad behavior, but it only brought you sadness, anxiety, and a deep sense of unfulfillment.

You know that you can't go on living like this, consumed by everybody else's lives, depleted because of constantly taking on their emotions and thoughts as your responsibility. It's time you listened to yourself, reflected on your own dreams and passions, and unleashed your marvelous inner self!

Chapter 9

Step 9: Grieving the Loss of Unhealthy Behavior and Letting Go

Think of your unhealthy behavior in terms of the different stages of grief. Throughout this book, you've probably been on a rollercoaster of emotions and countless shaking realizations. You've learned where your lack of boundaries comes from, why you have difficulty saying 'no' to others, how you ended up in codependent relationships, what made you become a compulsive people-pleaser, and why you've only existed through other people thus far.

However, you've also learned how to establish healthier boundaries, what to do to become more assertive, the best ways to deal with difficult or toxic people who keep violating your boundaries, how to break the pattern of people-pleasing and overcome the cycle of codependency, but most importantly how to stand in your truth and honor your authentic self. Now let's take a closer look at all that you've been through and how far you've come.

Denial

Examine a day in your life months ago, or even years ago, before you were even aware of your unhealthy behavior and poor choices. You were probably exhausted, undervalued, and often taken advantage of. Yet you never stopped to question the kind of treatment you received from others.

You took on all of your responsibilities, then some more, you worked on catering to the needs and desires of people around you, you wanted to establish yourself as the 'ride-or-die' type of friend, or as the partner who will always be there no matter what, the supportive sister, the fun mother, the friendly neighbor, the productive employee, the helpful coworker, and so on...

One commitment after the other, one engagement after the other, sleep deprivation slowly catching up on you, all those suppressed emotions bubbling underneath an immaculate surface. You didn't even acknowledge there was something wrong or iffy about your unsustainable lifestyle.

So whenever you'd get a comment from your partner or a friend that gently hints at the fact you're a people-pleaser, you're quick to throw your head back in laughter, dismiss their words, and change the subject.

Anger

Whether it's an abrupt wake-up call or a sudden realization, it finally dawns on you that other people's remarks are actually true. Maybe you are a pushover, maybe you are a people-pleaser, maybe you are a yes-man, a doormat, a weakling, a nonentity...

So you sit and begin reevaluating everything in retrospect with this newly uncovered 'evidence'. You over-analyze every conversation you've ever had, scanning for hints that show you're actually all of those things. You reflect on every failed relationship you've had, on your toxic family members, on your berating friends, on your overbearing sister.

You think and think and think. Then after putting everything through scrutiny, you finally realize that you actually have porous boundaries, that you always overwork yourself to the point of exhaustion to accommodate others, that you always put their needs way above yours, that your inability to speak your truth has led you to make some questionable choices.

Then suddenly, you're angry. You're angry with yourself, with the world, with the people you thought loved you unconditionally, with the universe even. Why did you even let go of yourself this far? How can others have the audacity to criticize you when all you've ever done is offer them love, affection, and emotional support?

So you lash out. You unleash all of those suppressed feelings of resentment and frustration, you want everyone to feel exactly like you do, you blame others for how and where you've ended up. You swear to yourself, you will never indulge anyone let alone give them permission to walk all over you. You feel like blasting your deafening thunderous rage, screaming at the top of your lungs "look what you've turned me into".

Bargaining

After blowing up on someone randomly, your anger dissipates to let room for guilt to settle in. You begin to regret yelling at that poor person who happened to be in your way without any apparent reason. Then you find yourself contemplating the "what ifs".

What if I had healthier boundaries? What if I were more assertive? What if I had the ability to say 'no' when I wanted to? What if I weren't so codependent? What if I didn't put other people's happiness above my own?

What if I knew how to exist on my own without needing external validation and approval? What if I were more authentic and truer to who I am? What if I had a better understanding of responsibilities? What if I could separate other people's lives from my own? ...

Following that is a cycle of 'if onlys'. So you start to contemplate what your life could have been, where you could have ended up, if only you made the right choices. Then bargaining begins. "I would definitely give this up if I could ...".

You wish you could return back in time to fix what's been damaged, but you can't, so you jump to the next best thing, which is getting what you want in exchange for sacrificing something else. You begin to negotiate with the hurt and pain you've accumulated, hoping this will lead you to a better version of yourself.

Depression

When you realize the past remains unchanged, that you can't do anything to erase the hurt, pain, and suffering you've caused as well as that which has been done to you, you suddenly find yourself in a fog of sadness, completely withdrawn from the world, and unable to progress.

You retreat far back into your own bubble and contemplate how any attempts on your part to redeem yourself are just going to be pointless at this moment in your life. So this will most likely be a period of isolation -a rare occurrence that is- for you to process this flux of information and reflect on your past self.

Acceptance

Now that you've taken the time to examine your unhealthy choices throughout this book, you probably feel calmer and more welcoming of this new reality knowing that you have the power to change it and move forward with your life.

You've managed to build a strong sense of self-awareness, you've dug deep to uncover your truth, you've done a personal inventory to assess who you are, and you're ready to start putting the strategies you've discovered to use.

While your journey of self-acceptance has just begun, you can tread safely knowing that through practice you will develop the level of assertiveness you needed to start making healthier choices.

Now that you're fully equipped to tackle whatever challenges lie ahead, you're prepared to start living a vital life, one that doesn't suppress who you are but rather shines the spotlight on your singularity and authenticity.

Release and Reconstruction

You're at a much better place now, which means you're ready to let go of the hurt, pain, and judgment you've been carrying all this time. Now, you can release all that built-up resentment, anger, and frustration to create more space for the things that matter, the things that will redirect you towards a life of joy, passion, and contentment.

This is the end of your grief, from here on out, you don't have to grieve the loss of making unhealthy choices anymore. You've been stuck, you've been taken advantage of, you've been exploited, but you've learned from those experiences, and most importantly you've grown.

Now is the time to thrive and flourish, to let your true self shine, to unleash your full potential. Release all of that negative energy and liberate yourself from your past. You're here, you're alive, the only thing that matters is the present moment and what you choose to make of it.

Conclusion

When you first picked up this book, you were probably feeling stuck, uninspired, and most likely exhausted. Actively going out of one's way to please others can be mentally and emotionally taxing, especially when those people prove to be incredibly difficult or toxic. So whatever you do never seems to be enough.

Taking responsibility for the needs wants, and feelings of the people around you is a never-ending task. You always think to yourself that there's room for improvement, that you could be doing more, offering more, giving more...

Yet, as the days go by, you find yourself becoming gradually more resentful and angrier at everyone around you simply because they don't work just as hard to accommodate you. So you feel like you put everyone else above yourself, except it's almost like you're at the very bottom of others' list of priorities.

Now that you've taken the time to examine your initial situation using this book as an outsider lens or objective perspective, you know that boundaries are at the center of everything. You can't learn how to say 'no' without healthy boundaries.

You can't break the cycle of people-pleasing without healthy boundaries. You can't overcome your codependency and learn to separate your life from other people's lives without, you guessed it, healthy boundaries.

Now, you know better than to suppress your thoughts, feelings, and emotions to make somebody else happy. You know better than to let others take advantage of you and deplete your precious resources. It's time to start taking care of yourself by implementing the tips and strategies mentioned in this book into your daily life.

It's never too late to start living your truth and honoring your values. This is your chance, so take it and make the most of your life, something grand, monumental, that goes beyond the guilt, shame, anger, and exasperation.

It all comes down to the steps you choose to take from here on out. So stay focused on what lies ahead and get yourself out of your mind and into the real world. You already have all the skills in your arsenal, you just need to nurture them. Be bold and dare to make the sacred commitment to yourself!

About the Author

Dr. Sheila Harris-Fitzpatrick is an Executive Clinical Director and founder of the Relationship Counseling & Psychotherapy Services and the Relationship Experts Academy, education and training center. She has worked and trained in California as well as Illinois. She is an educator first and also a coach and licensed professional therapist. Sheila's expertise is in grief coaching, relationship counseling and life transitions. She uses the way we connect in relationships to empower individuals and couples to have a life of fulfillment and happiness. Sheila has a passion for her work with adults and families helping them identify their gifts, talents, strengths, and struggles through life-altering events to find their authentic self to communicate, set boundaries and resolve conflict in pursuance of healthy relationships.

Find out more about, Dr. Sheila Harris-Fitzpatrick, Relationship Expert, Therapist and Entrepreneur at drsheilaharris.com

Dr. Sheila

HARRIS-FITZPATRICK
RELATIONSHIP EXPERT,
THERAPIST & ENTREPRENEUR